COLORFUL
MINDS

TIPS FOR
MANAGING
YOUR EMOTIONS

FUSION

The Blue Book

What to Do When You're Sad

by
William Anthony

BEARPORT
PUBLISHING

Minneapolis, Minnesota

Credits
Cover and throughout - Ekaterina Kapranova, Beatriz
Gascon J. 2 - NLshop. 8 - Jes2u.photo, 12 -Andyworks,
13 - kali9, 5 - NUM LPPHOTO, 18 - Vitaly Zorkin,
19 - tsaplia, Nata Kuprova, Reinbow Cake, Vera Serg,
Masha Kosorotikova. 20 - alexmak7, 21 - metrometro,
24-25 - OLENA KUZNIETSOVA. 27 - Premiumvectors.
30 - NLshop. Additional illustrations by Danielle
Webster-Jones. All images courtesy of Shutterstock.com.
With thanks to Getty Images, Thinkstock Photo
and iStockphoto.

Library of Congress Cataloging-in-Publication Data is available
at www.loc.gov or upon request from the publisher.

ISBN: 978-1-64747-578-9 (hardcover)
ISBN: 978-1-64747-583-3 (paperback)
ISBN: 978-1-64747-588-8 (ebook)

© 2022 Booklife Publishing

This edition is published by arrangement with Booklife
Publishing.

For more information, write to Bearport Publishing, 5357 Penn
Avenue South, Minneapolis, MN 55419. Printed in the United
States of America.

For more
The Blue Book activities:

1. Go to **www.factsurfer.com**

2. Enter "**Blue Book**" into the search box.

3. Click on the cover of this book
to see a list of activities.

CONTENTS

Imagine a Rainbow 4

To Infinity — and Breathe On! 6

Get Active! 8

The Thought Savers 10

Mindful Nature 12

Memory Box 14

The Monster Match. 16

Super You. 18

Little Ideas. 20

Feeling Better? 22

Glossary 24

Index 24

IMAGINE A RAINBOW

Red is angry.

Orange is for when I feel shy.

Feeling worried!

Green is scared.

The rainbow has a color for every feeling. Sometimes, one color shines brighter than the others.

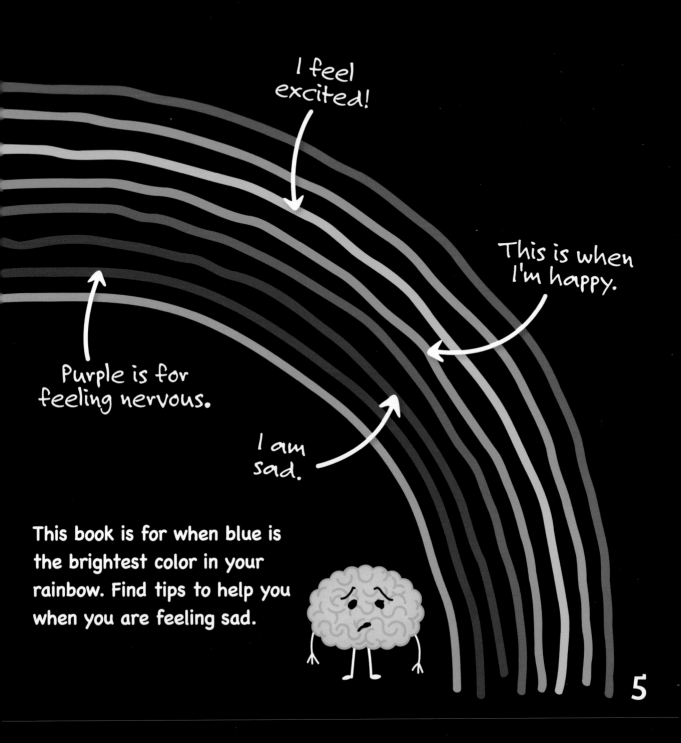

This book is for when blue is the brightest color in your rainbow. Find tips to help you when you are feeling sad.

TO INFINITY—
AND BREATHE ON!

We all show sadness in different ways.

If you are crying
and find it hard to
breathe, try this . . .

Slowly trace the path of the
arrows on the next page
with your finger. When you
trace the left side, breathe in.
When you trace the right side,
breathe out.

BREATHE IN

BREATHE OUT

GET ACTIVE!

When we are sad, **exercise** might be the last thing on our minds!

But exercise makes our bodies let out something in our brains that helps us feel happier and more hopeful.

TOP TIP!
Put on some music while you exercise!

Let's get moving!

STEP 1:
Do 10
jumping jacks!

STEP 2:
Run in place for
10 seconds!

STEP 3:
Do 10 big
arm circles!

STEP 4:
Breathe slowly and deeply
for 30 seconds.

THE THOUGHT SAVERS

Have you ever needed to talk to someone but it felt too hard?

Meet the thought savers.

They save all the thoughts you give them.

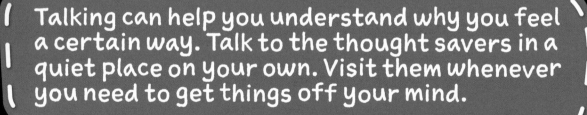

Talking can help you understand why you feel a certain way. Talk to the thought savers in a quiet place on your own. Visit them whenever you need to get things off your mind.

Tell them anything you'd like. Start with how you're feeling today and why.

MINDFUL NATURE

Spending time in nature can help us when we feel sad.

Being **mindful** is about noticing the things happening right now.

Take a trip to the park or your backyard. Try to notice things around you by using each of your senses. Take as long as you want.

TOP TIP!

Get an adult's permission before you go outside. Better yet, bring them with you!

MEMORY BOX

Sometimes people we love might die or move far away. This can make us feel very sad for a long time.

Making a memory box is a good way to remember someone. Grab an old box and fill it with things that remind you of the person who is no longer with you.

Things will begin to feel better before long. In the meantime, your box will help you look back on happy memories.

Here are some things you could put in your memory box!

A book you read together

A photo

Something from a special day you had with them

Something that was theirs

A drawing you did of them

Something they gave you

15

THE MONSTER MATCH

Emotions can be tricky to understand, and it isn't always easy to find something that helps you feel better.

I FEEL . . .

Lonely

Heartbroken

Disappointed

Low

Sad

TOP TIP!

Try matching monsters to find the best answers for you!

Maybe these monsters can help! Find a monster on the left page with a sign that says how you are feeling. Then, match it up with a way to respond to the feeling.

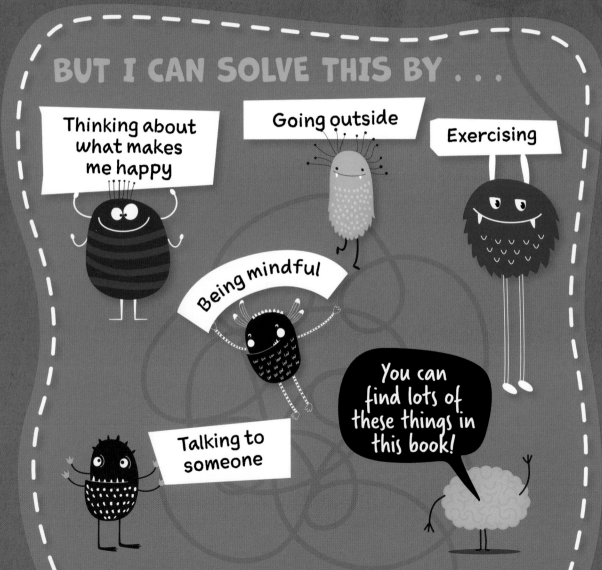

SUPER YOU

Sometimes we might cry, shout at other people, or hide from everyone. When we've calmed down, we might feel silly. That's okay!

When we feel like this, it is important to remember how super we are!

Get a trusted adult or friend and follow the steps on the next page together.

18

STEP 1:

Grab some pencils and paper.

STEP 2:

Write or draw something you are good at or why people like you. Don't let the other person see!

STEP 3:

Ask the other person to do the same thing about you. Don't look at their paper!

STEP 4:

When you are both finished, show each other!

LITTLE IDEAS

There are lots of little tips and tricks you can use when you feel sad.

BE CREATIVE

If you don't feel like talking, get **creative**. Try drawing something that shows how you feel.

TO-DO LIST

Make a list of things you need to do. This will get you moving.

KEEP A JOURNAL

Writing in a **journal** is a good way to get things off your mind.

CALM MUSIC

Listen to some calming music.

TAKE A WALK

Getting outside can put you in a better mood. Go for a walk with an adult.

FEELING BETTER?

Which tip worked best for you? Why do you think that is?

If you feel better, now is a good time to think about what made you feel sad and why. How might you handle things the next time you feel sad?

Remember, you are like everyone else. We all have colorful minds.

Every feeling you have is important!
This book will still be here

whenever

you need it.

GLOSSARY

creative having the ability to make new things or think of new ideas

disappointed feeling sad because something was not as good as you thought it might be

emotions strong feelings

exercise movements that make you strong and healthy

journal a book in which you write down your thoughts

mindful being aware of what is happening in the present moment

INDEX

breathing 6–7, 9
crying 6, 18
exercise 8, 17
memories 14–15
mindfulness 12, 17

music 8, 21
nature 12
senses 12
talking 10–11, 17, 20